Transparent Therapy

Dedicated to my brother Brandon Tyree Donley

Transparent Therapy

EDEN

I've seen beauty before

But yours has a distinction

Like different hues

Of the same color blue

In you

I see the fashion of God's artistry

Beneath the contour lines

Beautiful brown eyes

Lies this unique balance

Its like I'm looking at the quintessence of beauty

where confidence and intelligence inhabits

It's obvious your outer thing

But it's your conversation I find interesting

The breath of fresh air you bring

I find irresistibly refreshing

Experience tells me

Attraction ain't supposed to happen this quick

Because there's always this sense of complexity in the mix

When dealing with male female relationships

But the feeling of transparency I get

When we spend time

Is on par with the newness I feel

When I look into my daughter's eyes

So indeed

If we decide to cross the line

That which lies between time

And this finite rhyme

I believe would tell of a not too distant future

Existing between you and I

With the sky as our outline

And in between an endless bounty

I'm convinced there is nobody

More perfect for me than you

And if you give me the chance too

I will prove the same to be true

There is no man on this Earth

More perfect than me for you

Essentially consenting paramour

Scented colognes and pheromones

The pull of unexplainable impulses

Existing in perpetuity

Subtle ambiguity

Where we can fan the flames of ember and fire

Fueling our endless desires

Ambivalent

Beautiful and innocent

Full of zeal and tepidness

Ripe with exuberance and brilliance

You constantly hurt me

I want out

I won't carry your baggage any longer

I don't want to be angry anymore

I want to be stronger

At a time when I feel safest alone

When I'm around people their issues remind me

While I may not be perfect

The safest company is still my own

I have no business looking at you the way I do

I'm lying to myself in order to hide the truth

Despite being with someone else

It's clear to me the woman I want to be with is you

In the midst of societal delusions

and absent morals

It'll be our young people

who bring about better days

and brighter tomorrows

There's no worse feeling than believing the love you give her is enough

Only to realize it isn't and perhaps never was

Wakanda Inspired

For being a realization of a place we've only ever seen in our dreams

For depicting the diaspora, Pan-Africa futurism for the first time on the big screen

For enriching the images of our people revealing our majesty without reservation

For pulling traditions from real-life nations projecting our culture without any purpose or evasion

For providing representation cinema often lacks

For saying a man can be a superhero and king

And still be one hundred percent black

Undeniable chemistry

Positive energy

Existing comfortably in a space of

Laughter and rich conversation

Completely present

No hesitance

reciprocity on both sides

Not wasting one second

Most women spend their whole lives

And never get to experience a man who feels secure
enough in himself to not only protect her

but support her every dream

My Soul

If I could sing you a song

I would sing you my soul

Of all the women in all the houses

There is no doubt that this is my home

This is where I want to be

And this is where I belong

She can spend all day and offer all she like

But if she isn't you

Then she ain't my type

I like strong women like

Phenomenal women like you

Black women like you

While there exists this cynicism among black sistas that all the good black men are taken

That's just untrue

Because I'm standing right here

And I've been waiting you

You don't know it yet

But you've been waiting on me

The thing you wrote in your dairy God he let me see

So while I may seem unfamiliar when you look at me

The only thing I see when I look at you is destiny

The realization that a lie was packaged

And sold as love

Took a dove

And turned her into a vulture

You and I are one even

Like Adam and Eve in the Garden of Eden

Lay your head on my chest

And you'll hear not only mine

But you'll hear the heart of God beating

I opened up to you

Revealing the disparity in all my character flaws

Yet without complete understanding

You embraced and accommodated them all

Past trauma that creates and dictates how we feel

Should only be examined to manifest a circumstance
for which we can heal

One can either use how they feel to allow pain to fester
and rot

Or they can take control and make the past what it was
meant to be

A testimony or an after thought

A spirit that shines bright

dissipates darkness in the human soul

It illuminates a path for others

When feel like they're all alone

I want my daughter to believe she's worthy

That's she has the capability to craft her own narrative

And be the director of her own story

I've tried so hard

For so long

To be strong for this relationship

But the trip you keep taking me on

Has drawn on for too long

From a hurt I cannot fix

No matter how many times I try to make amends

I cannot win because love is a losing game

And no matter how much I change you clearly see me as the same

It's as though the person you see in me

In your mind

Is the only person you'll allow me to be

Growth is the result of pain

Experience gained

From the derivatives of heartache

The willingness to embrace mistakes

And the lessons of subsequent shame

God bring me closer to illumination

Stretch me along the sky

Reveal a better part of my nature

Allow me to see the world from your eyes

Lazy dreamers' egos age like worn clothes

Black kids institutionalized marred by an inferior complex

Commercialization of black ghettos has turned our pain into a product that trends

Incentivizing our kids that success comes by remaining in a constant state of descent

You can be blind to who a person is because of their lies and outward disguise

But if you pay close enough attention you'll see who they are every time

I thought about you so much today

I truly missed you all day today

I love you more each day I'm away

Before I sleep for you I pray

I wish you more reachable peace today

I wish you lots of unspeakable joy today

I wish I could be with you to say

I'm sorry for what I did yesterday

The inclination to hold my tongue

The thing that says to me tell her what she wants to hear so she doesn't run

That kind of thing

That kind of thinking that has me undone

Is the very thing that has me doing things with you that with no other woman I have ever done

How'd u sleep last night?

Was it pleasant?

Where'd you go when you sleep?

Was it heaven?

If history's records say the perfect number is 7

Then so too

God's perfect letter must be U

Like a house is not a home

This world is but a room

This body a tomb

Until words give it life

I will not wake 'til you tell me you love me

Not until you rest me in your curves

A real woman knows that God didn't just give her
power between her legs,

But he gave her power in her words

By its very definition and meaning the nature of a
woman's tonality

Completely warps a man's mentality

The discouragement and fear that extends from society
stay

Only become reinforced when women begin to stray
and say things that tear us down to our very core

Like a sickness or malignant sore

Your words have the ability to makes us soar

Or to bring us to ours knees

These words are simply a metaphor in order to get you
to see

That we need you

To see past the foolishness the world puts us through

And we'll continue to endure so long as we can put you on that pedestal

Where you and our children can make it through

And so I say to you:

Without so much as a tear

I will lie here

Content to die here

Until I hear

I cannot live without you

I will never doubt you

I trust you

Our children they need you

I could never ever replace you

True love lies somewhere between rage and serenity

The antithesis of anonymity

Exists on the paved roads of pain filled memories

Lodged amid warm thoughts of childlike fantasies

For women it's a strong masculinity

For men it's an infinite dependability on a woman who is a nurturer and a lover

A best friend when there is no other

A confidant

Someone who's share and keeps the insecurities of your thinking buried deep where nobody can find it

This person carries a light so high that no one can outshine it

In a life where we are born with no favors no waivers that lessen the life lessons of the environments we live in

Like God forgave yours

Give your heart a break and let love make amends for the sin of the world

And those that hurt you those that hit you those abused you

They were wrong but I pray you let me sing you a song that heals you

and fills you will a joy that you cannot explain

A love that confounds every theory and excuse you have not to love again

It's doesn't matter how you found it or whether you deserve it

All that matter is that you are worth it

True love lies in the pain we know and the connection we seek

Everything in between is simply pressure we put on ourselves to be strong but really makes us weak

End of Poem

My spirit longs to live in the glory

Of your presence

The heavens and everything that you made so wonderfully

I humbly come before thee to ask thee if I can be amongst
those whom you call friend

I want my commitment to come before the end

I want to live in the assurance my salvation covers me
triumphantly over my sin

In doing so I hope to join my brothers and sisters who have
given theirs live too

I am nothing without you

The Who and The What about me is Nil

Grant me the serenity to find Peace so finally the Peace
inside of me can be still

I know the only place to find true peace is inside your will

I am here for one reason

To confess that I am a heathen

To admit that I can't do this on my own

I want to be rid of this sick feeling, of feeling alone

I don't care where you take me Lord just take me along

And after we're home

I pray that you breathe new life into these dry bones

Queen Lover

Mother of the black womb

Wake from your nightmares, the tears, and the rape wounds

The day will arrive soon

When we stride to the slave tombs

With our heads held high and celebrate what we came through

Long days I say

Long days, say

Sing along

My way goes on and on and on…

These past few days have been nothing but rainy days

Echoes of burdens weigh on my subconscious

Bellows of no Zzzzs keeps me sleepless in Seattle

Redundancy surrounds me

These sounds you hear is of sulk soaking this heavily
drenched soul

For just one minute of me time

For peace of mind I would give anything

You see it's hard to hear anything

Because while I'm listening to you I'm still listening for my
kids

I close my lids and wonder to myself is this all there is

I'm starting to feel bitterness toward my seeds because of
my condition

I know it's not their fault but you see they are the reflection
of all my bad decisions

And this thankless job of no recognition

Makes me feel like all my sacrifices are in vain

I'm sick of hearing "God is Good just maintain"

Trying to remain sane while raising these kids, its damn near impossible

It seems I'm just a rerun of my own about humble beginnings

But now between this 2-year old's teething and early morning feedings

To me it seems like my life is pointed toward an even worse ending

I try so hard because I don't want my kids to see me like this

But with my baby daddy not willing to assist

My faith is nonexistent

I feel worthless, like a piece of shit

And after all my attempts to get ahead I'm barely making it

Some days I feel like I just can't take it

So long days, yeah

Very long days

Except I sing alone my way goes on and on and on

She thought she was ready

But the weight of having a good man got a little too heavy

So wrapped in her head

She did what any scared woman would've did

She ran from that good man

Back into the arms of a thug she was comfortable with

A waste of time

Bequeathed by their own demise

Spend more time gossiping about my life than improving their own lives

If they only knew God's hand was upon me

His purpose by design

They'd cease making up these stories

These calculated lies

I am precious

Beauty flows out of me like water

Your idea of who I am is beyond useless

I belong to my Father

And he thinks I am wonderful

He tells everyday

His word anchors my confidence

I'm beautiful because he says I am

I don't care what you think of me

Your opinion matters not

You try to convince me its cold outside when it's not

I've got my whole life ahead of me

My future is so bright

Negativity is the dimmer of dreams and Love lights my path

I will never let you kill my self-esteem

I cherished you so much I married you

Every day I wake up next to you I reaffirm my commitment to you

I wanted to spend the rest of my life with you

All these years later I still do

She was more shine than the eyes could see

She was more intellect than the mind could think

She was the Garden of Eden

Creation untarnished

She was like a new Cadillac with a fresh varnish

I'm talking sensual magic

Her body, her language

She exuded a confidence that was unapologetic

She's was matchless

Like an angel fell from the sky

A sweet onion

The more I looked at this woman the more I wanted to cry

Her walk was like harmony

A melodic line of scat

Near her cool cats turned to fools that could never keep their cool together

Maybe it was her African-American

Sandy beach complexion

Or maybe it was the impression left by the strength of her presence

Either way both of her parents ought to receive merits

For having a daughter so fine

A dime

With a body as if it were scripted line by line

Wool hair, thick thighs, no weave, brown eyes

She was born straight out of a fantasy

A Black Mona Lisa brought forth to reality

End of Poem

I am living outside of my body experiencing living for the first time

Wrapped in a love that hypnotized my mind

I'm high

Paralyzed when I'm inside you

When I'm with you I'm not burdened by unrealistic expectations and impracticality

I can breathe easy because when I turn that key and open that door I'm home

Vulnerable to the world I'm naked

But when I'm with you I'm covered and clothed

I'm whole

I couldn't ask for a more perfect person to connect my life too

The weight of the world is a cross worth bearing, all because I'm coming home to you

Humility is a thorned crown

It'll break you down

Humility confounds arrogance

And runs a fool it into the ground

Raising kids in a system

Centered and commissioned

On putting young black bodies in a grave or in a penal system

For a black mother there is but one decision

To have the most impact

On whom the odds are already stacked

While other mothers worry about keeping their kids on the straight and narrow

A black mother has to contend with their kids being swallowed by the streets or staring down a cop's gun barrow

Historical levels of low education in urban communities persist

Massive rates of unemployment

Increased prison rates make for better business

The world witnesses police brutality and fatalities of black families

And no one is held accountable

Except the victim

Thoughts

Mindless texts

Posts ending with emojis and hashtags

Billions of words randomly tweeted out

Ideas and conceptions

Time and space attaching themselves to certain perceptions

Relevancy belongs to truth being spoken through reality and fantasy

I'm standing

Waiting for my big break

Faithfully

Waiting for fate

To meet me

At this crossroads of clarity

Waiting while I bear my cross barely

Giving all that I've got

My soul's ready to give in

Closed door after closed door

Rejection from there to here

Down my cheek

Streams the first of many tears

I wonder if fate even knows I'm here

Do's and don'ts

Manufactured fronts

Hallowed hellos

And awkward goodbyes

Comfort exists within these walls of isolation

Safety and insulation from outside infiltration makes for peace and quiet

Silence to noise and distractions

Perceptions expectations for how we ought to be

How we ought to act

How we ought to believe

They hate me

Without cause

All for their own

Righteous applause

If you listen closely

You can read my mind

All it takes is effort

All it takes is time

Theoretical problems

Social validations that never pass

Quantifiable shapes over gaps that never fit

Thoughts on any and everything

Self-created problems that never exist

Control is an ism

A psychological mechanism

That binds you to whatever it wants you to do

As long as you lack the inability

To see responsibility

As something other than someone else telling you what to do

You lose

The great need for forgiveness is an order of life

An adage of the spirit of reciprocity

That lies and thrives on the cyclical behavior of our own

The finiteness of our lives tells us that perfection escapes us

Emotionally we're complex

Flaw-full creatures of an imperfect nature

Finding every reason

To mount our opinions and judgments on others so we can escape our own dread

By calling someone else's life

The night of the living dead

We see ourselves as clean instead of the filthy persons we are

Because it allows us to see everyone else's trouble more easily

But are we not all troubled

Have we not all in our own ways

In our own minds

Each of us at different times

Needed God to rewind

Or fast forward past time

So could we could get past that thing or two

We don't want anybody else to see

Or is it just me

Am I the only one

Who's book of life is chapter after chapter full of God's grace

Am I the only one

Who's hand God gave when I was damn near in my grave

You look down on others

But when it was us that were scathed

Did he not show compassion

And grace

And mercy

And love

And peace

Salvation

And kindness

Forgiving someone isn't all of a sudden suffering from a case of blindness

No, it's a change of the heart

Spiritual mindedness

Where the focus is about putting anger and bitterness aside

Forgiveness is not having to hide

Many people feel they've been so wronged

Angry for so long

They hate the world

And don't know why

End of Poem

Trapped in the night

In the wilderness stranded

Searching for the meaning of life

A long tear streamed down the face of the once proud arrogant prince

He who had all the answers since an early age has since aged and the stage he finds himself is packed with riddles that leave his thoughts crippled by simple questions like?

When was the last time you were happy?

The gravity of the questions creates a hesitation in his thought process

Concepts that leave him confounded, dumbfounded

Sinking deep in the recess of his own psycho analytic mess

Crooked streams trail off as she fell beneath the waterfall

What seemed like hours were only seconds

Howls drowned out by hollow winds in a deep silence

Distorted voices speak loudly to her subconscious

I thought about you so much today

I truly missed you all day today

I love you more each day I'm away

Before I sleep for you I pray

I wish you more reachable peace today

I wish you unspeakable joy today

I wish I could be with you to say

I'm sorry for what I did yesterday

Sometimes in my consciousness

I feel very little confidence

Feelings of low self-esteem

I continually have to fight against

I know my heart has lied before

But now it speaks truth

Ways of life brought forth by changes made to heal the places I've been hurt the most

In essence my very being was being tested

By the sweetest effervescent

Intertwining my soul with a spirit not of my own

Feelings of pleasure my heart has never known

Endless emotions with my minds thoughts driven like waves in the ocean

But I ignored them

All my life I've dreamed of meeting a love designed with no lies

No deceptions

A love made alive

Made just for me

Once I found this charity I'd cherish for all of eternity

But life didn't seem to dream the same manner as me

Then just as I gave up looking for love

A greater love found me

Caught off guard it touched my heart

It softened something that once was hardened

My eyes became blurry

My arms wouldn't move

I couldn't fathom the words that came from my lips

It felt as though an angel came from heaven and gave my soul a kiss

I didn't know love was made to feel like this

Surely God knew my heart when He granted me this one wish

To love and be loved unconditionally

The inclination to hold my tongue

The thing that says to me tell her what she wants to hear so that she doesn't run

That kind of thing

That kind of thinking that has me undone

Is the very thing that has me doing things with you that with no other woman has ever been done

She was more shine than the eyes could see

She was more intellect than the mind could think

Like Eve from Eden

Creation untarnished

She was like a new Caddy with a fresh varnish

I'm talking sensual magic

Her body, her language

She exuded a cool that was unapologetic

She was matchless

Like an angel fell from the sky

A sweet onion

The more I looked at this woman the more I wanted to cry

Her walk was like harmony

A melodic line of scat

Near her cool cats turned to fools that could never keep their cool together

I don't know maybe it was her African-American sandy beach complexion

Or maybe it was just the heir left by her very presence

Either way both of her parents ought to receive merits for having a daughter so fine

I'm talking a dime

With a body as if it were scripted line by line

Wool hair, thick thighs, fat ass, brown eyes

She was a portrait born straight out of a fantasy

A Black Mona Lisa brought forth to reality

End of Poem

Undeniable energy

Electricity every time we touch

A rush

Waves of exhilaration

Impatient to be in each other's presence

The precursor to serendipity

Best friends

Lovers

Kindred spirits who find their way back to each other

Stars that orbit each other's solar systems

Existing parts of the soul no one else knew existed

It reminds me of you the most

A sweetness that swells in the smell of a rose

I can't put my finger on it

But it

The Essence of your intellect

The Harmony of your cleverness

The Strength of your confidence

It makes me want you more

Like an orchestra noire

Playing a melody

That keeps me standing

And clapping

"Encore!"

It lets me know you're real

An indistinguishable signature

Beautiful & Nameless

It's the core of you

I like to call Fragrance

I'm closer to grace than I've ever been

I'm grateful sin doesn't control my life like it did back when

Before I found joy, found peace

Glory to the most high God who supplies my every need

From the pain I carried around my neck like a leash

To the pile of pride I was buried beneath

I questioned myself if I would ever be free

In him I know I'm no longer condemned

There is nothing to gain by being away from him

My life is empty being away from him

If you ask me who do I love most my answer is always Him

Pondering on everything I've been given

How I've been forgiven

People I've taken for granted

Loves I've lost

Love I've gained

Success I accumulated over time

Mistakes I've made

Near misses

Near death experiences

Sitting here marveling on the life I've lived

So thankful

Anticipating the life, I still have left to finish

Who I AM

You accept it

With no prerequisite

I get to bend

Fallback and get up again

Brush off the dust of my mistakes

Without being made to feel like an ingrate

Your grace brings me into a headspace that provides me the room to recalibrate

With you I don't feel alone

Condoned or simply tolerated

Sunken deep in contention

Temporary healing

The band-aid of religion

To no avail

The veil was ripped away

The soul is missing

Catatonic

Locked in a spiritual prison

Earth tones

Rolled away stones

Pious righteous

Beautiful and strong

A rose blooms with no provocation

The morning rises not out of obligation

And like the rose and the morning with no hesitation

I want to express my appreciation, for you being in my life

Desperately creating distance between implicitness and consciousness

no care of time

submerging my desires with the textiles of sublime flight

peering out on the veracity

No agenda or ceiling

staying away from other people's expectations

Creating my own

bottoming out on my addiction of creating lies of the contradiction

Developing concepts that have no limitation, no end or depth

A disguise to breed pretense

Facts dismissed

Slick tongues slithering souls

Black crows journeying far and wide answering the coming of winter's toll

Converging different types of summations possibilities and conversions

Distracting thoughts diverging ideas

Immersing themselves in the depth of my amygdala

Nervousness and fear apprehend and stares at me

Weighing me down like disparate rain

So indeed

If we decide to cross the line

That which lies between time

And this finite rhyme

I believe would tell of a not too distant future

Existing between you and I

With the sky as our outline

And in between an endless bounty

I'm convinced there is nobody

More perfect for me than you

And if you give me the chance too

I will prove the same to be true

There is no man on this Earth

More perfect than me for you

Undeniably, there were days you though you would break

Abusive men you felt you'd never escape

There were people you imagine you could never relate

Insecurities you swore you would never embrace

A life you say wrought with so many mistakes

Became the epitome of strength humility and grace